FOR
AFTERWORD BY LOU ENGLE

THE DREAM SPEAKER

LEARNING GOD'S LEADERSHIP THROUGH
THE LANGUAGE OF DREAMS

CORRY ROBINSON

Copyright © 2020 by Corry Robinson

The Dream Speaker
By Corry Robinson

Printed in the United States of America

ISBN: 978-1-950810-06-2

All rights reserved. No part of this document may be reproduced or transmitted in any form, by any means (electronic, photocopying, recording, or otherwise) without the written permission of the author.

Bible quotations marked NASB are taken from the New American Standard Bible. Copyright © 1960, 1962, 1963, 1968, 1971, 1972, 1973, 1975, 1977, 1995 by The Lockman Foundation.

Bible quotations marked NIV are taken from the Holy Bible, New International Version®, NIV® Copyright ©1973, 1978, 1984, 2011 by Biblica, Inc.® Used by permission. All rights reserved worldwide.

Bible quotations marked KJV are taken from the King James Version of the Bible. Public domain.

Bible quotations marked GNT are taken from the Good News Translation. Copyright © 1992 by American Bible Society.

Bible quotations marked NLT are taken from the Holy Bible, New Living Translation. Copyright © 1996, 2004, 2015 by Tyndale House Foundation. Used by permission of Tyndale House Publishers, Inc., Carol Stream, Illinois 60188. All rights reserved.

Bible quotations marked ESV are taken from the The Holy Bible, English Standard Version. ESV® Text Edition: 2016. Copyright © 2001 by Crossway Bibles, a publishing ministry of Good News Publishers.

Bible quotations marked BSB are taken from the The Holy Bible, Berean Study Bible, BSB. Copyright © 2016, 2018 by Bible Hub. Used by Permission. All rights reserved worldwide.

Burning Ones Publishing
https://burningones.org

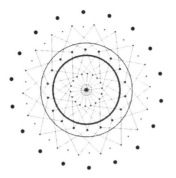

ACKNOWLEDGMENTS

To my Lord, Savior, and nearest Friend, Jesus Christ. You took me from my mother's womb and called me to Yourself. Words can never sufficiently express the love and gratitude I have for Your unending mercies and saving grace, and the fact of having the greatest privilege of knowing You intimately is beyond comprehension.

To my loving and amazing wife, Lakisha. After over twenty years of doing life and ministry together, and nearly fifteen years of marriage, I can honestly say I've never known a more devoted, caring, strong, and sacrificial person as you. You never cease to amaze me. Thank you for your love for Jesus and undying support for me through the years. Certainly life is better with you than without you! I love you!

To my pastor, father-in-law, and friend, Pastor Victor Morgan. Your example of love for Jesus and His Church is to be admired and imitated. Thank you for laboring and caring for the flock of God the way you do. Even as I write this, I reminisce of the many times you've encouraged me, rebuked me, challenged me, and showed me the right ways of God when I was prone to veer left. Everywhere I go, your words are always with me.

To my mother-in-law, Paula Morgan, for your many prayers and endless care for me through the years, I am eternally grateful. You carry such grace, kindness, and elegance. I am privileged to have married into your family.

To my Victorious Living Fellowship family, there is never any place compared to home. I wholeheartedly agree with King David when he said, "Lord, I have loved the habitation of thy house, and the place where thine honour dwelleth" (Psalm 26:8).

Lastly, to Lou Engle. Lou, thank you for sowing your life for the turning of our beloved nation. Thank you for demonstrating to generations, young and old, what it means to lay down one's life for the interests of God's heart and embrace the call to set oneself apart for the sake of seeing the borders of God's Kingdom established in the nations of the earth. Instead of monetizing encounters with the eternal realm as many

ACKNOWLEDGMENTS

do, I have witnessed as you have sold yourself as a slave to the purposes of God and this Gospel, and even to the selling of your possessions and your children's inheritance so the dream of God's heart concerning you could become reality. Lou, though you have no brick-and-mortar monument in the earth in the name of ministry, may the legacy of prayer, fasting, and dreaming God's dreams be as seeds in the earth, springing up into a fruitful harvest unto the coming of our Lord Jesus Christ!

DEDICATION

To my mother, Eunice. Thank you for instilling in me the value of my dreams! In so doing, you instructed me to be always listening for the voice of God in the night!

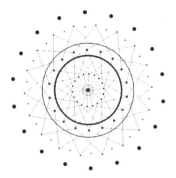

TABLE OF CONTENTS

Foreword		xiii
Introduction		xvii
Chapter One	A Sudden Interruption	27
Chapter Two	A Tale of Two Kings	39
Chapter Three	Ways in Which God Speaks	53
Chapter Four	Dreams and Revelation	59
Chapter Five	Dreams, Interpretation, and Prophecy	73
Chapter Six	The Journey into Revelation	83
Chapter Seven	Divine Understanding: The Key to Discerning Dreams	92
Chapter Eight	God's Word: Our Standard for Interpreting Dreams	97
Chapter Nine	From Joel 2 to Acts 2	115
Afterword		121
About the Author		127

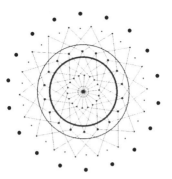

FOREWORD

I have had the privilege to know Corry Robinson for several years now. He is a friend. I consider him a brother. It has been a joy and an honor to be knitted to a man that walks in such a dynamic way with the Lord. For those who also know Corry, I am sure that you can attest to the real and powerful way that God's voice has been entrusted to him, and how that seems to energize those who find themselves in his presence.

I don't want to say that God has entrusted His voice to Corry in a way that seems exclusive to only his life. However, there is a truth I believe Corry has communicated throughout this book, and it is this—God's desire to speak to us may seem to come without charge. However, living a life that is devoted to growing in sensitivity to the voice of God and deepening in the experience and obedience to His voice will cost you everything.

Corry's life is a great example of a man that has labored before the Lord to develop the maturity in the areas that have been mentioned. God has entrusted His voice to Corry in a real, deep, and dynamic way because of the trust that He has been able to find in him as His son. It should be the joy and goal of our lives to develop such a place before the Lord.

Living a life that is devoted to growing in sensitivity to the voice of God and deepening in the experience and obedience to His voice will cost you everything.

In the development of learning God's voice and then attempting to navigate a life that is led by God's voice, it will be impossible not to consider the inclusion of dreams and visions. For God has communicated it Himself through a variety of prophetic vessels, and various moments of powerful preaching and utterances, that His goal is to fully unleash these realities into our lives.

Joel says that in the last days God's communication will include dreams and visions.[1] God, through Joel, is making it clear to us that in the age of the outpouring

---

[1] Joel 2:28, NASB

of the Holy Spirit, which is where you and I are today, that God will not just unveil His desire to speak to us and lead us by dreams and visions, but that it will also be a reality for us and a powerful distinction for our lives that have been filled by the power and presence of the Holy Spirit.

God wants to speak to you through dreams and visions. That much we know is true. However, no matter how true that may be, it doesn't mean that we are doing our part to believe it, receive it into full working reality in our lives, and then be led by it as a real source of divine communication.

Much of the history of my life and walk with the Lord makes absolutely no sense whatsoever unless you include the influence and leadership of God's voice through dreams and visions. And, not just include it, but also give it its proper and powerfully influential place. Dreams and visions have shaped much of my family's life, and we are grateful to the Lord for His desire and ability to communicate with us this way, for there is no telling where we may have been had we not had His voice in this manner and counted it precious to us.

I encourage you to take the journey that you find in the pages of this book that follow you as a divine appointment. Because of the content that has been shared in this book I believe with all of my heart that your life will potentially never be the same. Be encouraged as you glean from the life of a man that has opened up the treasure chest of God in his own heart and life to share with the rest of us the precious gems that have been revealed to him over years and years of walking with the Lord.

The Lord is longing to have a people for Himself that would be fully alive in Him to all of His ways. May you, like David writes in the psalms, be filled with a praise to God Most High for His beautiful way of bringing us instruction in the night![2] Get ready, oh wonderful dreamer, it's time!

Michael Dow
President, Burning Ones

---

[2] Ps 16:7, NASB

INTRODUCTION

As the age moves ever so close to its end, as if its pangs and contractions of seemingly myriads of crises nearly simultaneously crashing upon the earth, the voice of the Lord can, if we are not careful and watchful, be literally drowned out as humanity is overcome by the issues of the day. Society is on edge, as ethnic groups contend for dominance, and nations seek permanently fixed positions of power and control of the earth's resources. In the midst of such great unrest and distress of nations, is there a body of peace in the earth?

In such a confused world where that which was once commonly considered evil and abominable is now celebrated and encouraged, is there a voice of clarity crying out to the rest of society? Is there a prophet among us? According to the Bible, the answer to those legitimate questions is a resounding YES!

From the beginning of creation, God has had in His mind a means by which those who are born from above would be clear signs in the very heavens and lights that would rule the darkness. In the account of creation in Genesis, the God of all creation "separated the light from the darkness."[3] Thus, His intent from the start has been for there to be a complete separation from darkness. It is only in this way the light remains pure and unaffected by the darkness around it. In this historic hour of human history, one of the greatest issues of the day is that of sanctification and holiness, what it means and what it does not.

I believe we are entering into an age of unprecedented divine enlightenment in the Church of Jesus Christ, and that the arena of dreams is heaven's distribution for divine guidance. Therefore, it is my desire in this writing to lay a foundation for faith for the dream realm, as we dive into the depths of what the Scriptures have to say on such a topic.

---

[3] Gen 1:4, NASB

INTRODUCTION

There are many well-meaning people in the Body of Christ who are perplexed along with the world and have no ability to discern what the Lord is saying relative to their personal lives! Of course, we cannot open up the pages of the Bible and find chapter and verse detailing what we are to do with the rest of our lives here on this earth. If it were that easy, the world would be perfectly in order, and there would be no need for a Church through which the power of the Gospel of the coming Kingdom is preached. However, as we will soon see, the will of God is often veiled in mystery, which demands our attention as well as a willingness to mine out the mysteries concealed by Him.

The intent of *The Dream Speaker* is to incite the desire of the heart

I believe we are entering into an age of unprecedented divine enlightenment in the Church of Jesus Christ, and that the arena of dreams is heaven's distribution for divine guidance.

into a flaming frenzy to pursue the Living God whose glory it is to conceal Himself that He might be found. And finding Him is the prize, because attaining and restraining God puts the seeker in position to mine out the deep things of His heart through simply spending time fellowshipping with Him. Finding God is not cheap, and the process of pursuing Him will cost everything. But the benefits are far too numerous to count, and in fact are beyond our capacity to reason.

As it is written in 1 Corinthians chapter 2 verse 9, "eye has not seen, nor ear heard, the things which God hath prepared for them that love Him." He has, however, provided a way in which believers can lay hold of the things that are hidden in Him, and that way is, "by His Spirit."[4]

GIDEON AND HIS VICTORY OVER THE MIDIANITES

A clear and practical example of how a dream and its interpretation brought major blessing, benefit, and advancement to God's people can be seen in the life of Gideon in Judges chapter 7. Interestingly, there was apparently direct communication between the Lord and Gideon, which begs the question of, "Why did God need to use a dream in order to spring Gideon into action?" While the answer to that question is not entirely clear, what is evident is the instructive aspect of dreams and interpretation in this account of Judges chapter 7. As Paul tells Timothy, "ALL SCRIPTURE is God-breathed and is useful for teaching, rebuking, correcting and training (instruction) in righteousness."[5]

---

[4] 1 Cor 2:9-10, NASB
[5] 2 Tim 3:16, NIV

INTRODUCTION

In this particular account, God whittled Gideon's army down from thirty thousand to just three hundred. As they faced the reality of military engagement with the army of the Midianites, Gideon was instructed to take his servant with him down to the encampment of the Midianite army to listen to what they were saying amongst each other. To their utter astonishment, this is what they heard,

> "As Gideon arrived, a man was telling his friend about a dream. 'Behold, I had a dream,' he said, 'and I saw a loaf of barley bread come tumbling into the Midianite camp. It struck the tent so hard that the tent overturned and collapsed.' His friend replied: 'This is nothing less than the sword of Gideon son of Joash, the Israelite. God has delivered Midian and the whole camp into his hands.' **_When Gideon heard the dream and its interpretation_**, he bowed in worship. He returned to the camp of Israel and said, 'Get up, for the LORD has delivered the camp of Midian into your hands.' "[6]

Notice a few specific things here. First, the Midianites apparently placed a high priority on

---

[6] Judges 7:13-15, NIV emphasis added

dreams, insomuch that they were obviously shaken by the dream told in the camp! Would to God that we gave that level of priority to the dreams God gives. How much undue pain and misery would we be spared as we heeded the warnings and directives of the Lord given in the night season?

Second, if the barley cake dream was the sum total of the conversation in the camp, there would have been no cause for concern amongst the soldiers. The interpretation of the dream brought great gravity and clarity to the situation and gave Gideon the confidence necessary to overcome fear and be victorious in battle.

How much undue pain and misery would we be spared as we heeded the warnings and directives of the Lord given in the night season?

Third, Gideon DID THE DREAM! The interpretation of the dream provided practical, step-by-step instructions for a victorious conquest!

"Watch me and do as I do," Gideon said. "When I come to the outskirts of the camp, do exactly as I do. When I and all who are with me blow our trumpets, then you are also to blow your trumpets from all around the camp and shout, 'For the Lord and for Gideon!' "[7]

---

[7] Judges 7:17-18, BSB

INTRODUCTION

Exactly as the dream was interpreted, so Gideon did, and all his army imitated him. Thus, the entire nation was delivered from the hand of the oppressor through a dream and its interpretation.

Notice this sequence: God sent a dream, which was followed by skillful interpretation; the dream was received into the heart as being from the Lord (hence, Gideon's worship); and finally, a faith-filled response! Beloved ones, a single dream (and skillful interpretation) from the Lord is enough to completely decimate the power of oppressors and to remove their destructive influence from the life of anyone willing to simply believe, receive, and respond in obedience to divine instructions through the wisdom of the Spirit!

Because God's thoughts and ways are so much higher than ours, He must establish a bridge of translation, a method by which humanity can migrate from our finite world of reason to His infinite realm of revelation. This is precisely why it is imperative that we cultivate the skill of understanding and interpreting dreams given by the Holy Spirit! The most fundamental way to develop the ability to interpret dreams given by the Spirit is to draw near to God and to become well-versed in the mysteries of the Word of God, for therein is "hid all the treasures of wisdom and knowledge."[8]

---

[8] Col 2:3, KJV

The great patriarchs of the faith—Abraham, Isaac, Jacob, Joseph, Daniel, and all who were catapulted into exalted positions through divine dreams and interpretations, and used as catalysts to pivot culture in its most desperate and critical moments—were obviously both wholly devoted to the pursuit of the presence and will of God, and were given to the consumption *and* assimilation of His Word. As King David so rightly declared, "Thou through Thy commandments have made me wiser than mine enemies.... I have more understanding than all my teachers: for Thy testimonies are my meditation."[9]

The most fundamental way to develop the ability to interpret dreams given by the Spirit is to draw near to God and to become well-versed in the mysteries of the Word of God.

The invitation to meditate in the Scriptures, instead of mere study or memorization of Bible verses or even whole passages (both of which are good and helpful, but are insufficient ways for building a root system of the Word of God in the inner man) is God's primary method of developing the language of the Spirit in us. It is His "bridge of translation" (if you will) that moves us upward into the revelatory realms of heaven. As our

---

[9] Ps 119:98-99, KJV

INTRODUCTION

Lord Jesus extended an upward invitation to Nathaniel in John chapter 1 verse 51 when He said, "Ye shall see heaven open, and the angels of God ascending and descending upon the Son of man," we also have the same promise of ascension as we meditate in His Word! What a glorious expectation!

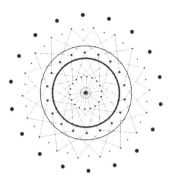

CHAPTER ONE

A SUDDEN INTERRUPTION

From a very young age, as far back as I can remember, I have always experienced a very active dream life. I can vividly recall dreams of flying through the atmosphere, soaring over cities, valleys, entire bodies of water. I'm unsure of what those dreams meant entirely, but they have been stamped on my memory without ever having to write them down. When I reached my late teens, however, it seems my dreams had significantly dissipated. My life had increasingly been given over to lasciviousness and wild living. Exposure to porn, violence, music videos, and every other medium of "entertainment" had so polluted my mind that it seems there was no room for anything else, let alone dreaming.

I began to seriously and vigorously pursue a career in singing in the mid 1990s, the revival decade of the pop music boy band era. I was always musically inclined. My mother tells me that I could hum a tune before I could stand on my own two feet—literally! Mother was always active in the church, and her mainstay was music ministry. She has a beautiful alto Mahalia-esque voice that would put the fear and awe of God in your heart as she bellowed old, Black Baptist spirituals and hymns.

As a newborn, there was no babysitter available to keep me during my mother's choir rehearsals at church, so she brought me along, stretching me out on a Baptist palette of linens while she and the Mount Tabor Primitive Baptist Adult Choir #1—as it was affectionately called—hammered out harmony parts to gospel numbers and songs from the hymnals. While lying there in the choir stand that doubled as a baptismal, I was baptized with psalms, hymns, spiritual songs, and African-American gospel music!

By the time I could walk, I was well able to hum a melody, and even harmonize a tune! Mother made well sure that I participated in every (and I mean EVERY) youth choir, young adult choir, Christmas and Easter program, summer camp choir, etc.; and if

A SUDDEN INTERRUPTION

there was a special gathering or convention that required a musical selection, I was a part of that too! Needless to say, by the time I reached my teenage years, I was a pretty well-rounded singer, and had added lite classical voice training when I was in fifth grade.

Something happened, however, to the awe and wonder of "church." I began to question within myself if what I knew to be "church" was in fact real when compared to the stories we were taught in Sunday school, or was there more to what our primitive family church put on display?

> **Was what I knew to be "church" real when compared to the stories we were taught in Sunday school, or was there more to what our primitive family church put on display?**

At the age of fourteen, I began to sing in my high school choir—both classical and black gospel—and others outside of the church began to notice that I had a voice. I must say, too, that the voice I had was not your typical fourteen-year-old tenor voice trying to settle in the valley of puberty; no, mine was atypical. In fact, it was so atypical, that for most of my young life, I was the young man in the soprano/alto section of EVERY choir I had EVER been in!

Before long, I was invited to sing with a group of guys, most of whom had graduated high school while

I was just a sophomore. There were six of us, and we quickly gained local notoriety, winning every talent contest we entered by displaying an uncanny ability to perform the song and dance, mostly without the need for musical instruments. We had won the favor of the main radio personality for Orlando's largest R&B radio station of that time, 102 Jamz's Bartel Bartel! Oh, we were BIG TIME…well…at least ghetto fabulous.

While touring local and regional venues, we eventually landed an opportunity to audition for what would be the modern-day equivalent of *The Voice* or *American Idol*—Ed McMahon's *Star Search*! The season's series of the show was to be broadcasted from Walt Disney World in Orlando, and we were sure we were well on our way to stardom. After all, we had made our mark on Central Florida, and it was just about time for us to "make it big."

As we arrived at the audition venue, which was the site of one of the large Disney resort hotels, we gathered in the hotel lobby, placed our keyboard (the ONLY instrument we had) on the floor, and began to harmonize one of our favorite songs. Little did we know, a record label executive was there in the lobby, and was listening in on our little rehearsal.

What was striking is that he was not there as a part of the *Star Search* festivities; he was on vacation with his family and was getting ready to turn in for the

A SUDDEN INTERRUPTION

night with his wife and children and was distracted by our singing. He was so impressed, he immediately introduced himself, invited us up to his hotel room, and offered to fly us up to New York to shop our talent at the major record labels in the city! Long story short, he did, we did, and the rest is history (as they say)! We signed a deal with Zumba, the publishing arm of Jive Records.

> **Depression began to set in as I realized that the dream of stardom, fame, riches, and notoriety was escaping my grip.**

Fast-forward a few years to 1997. The band had broken up after having major disagreements, some of the older guys had gotten married and started families, and the realities of "adulting" begin to set in, which meant it was time to get a real job! I, on the other hand, was the youngest of the gang, and had several opportunities to further my career as a recording artist. I found myself writing and recording with various artists and producers, and had several songs thought by many to be potential hit records.

Before long, however, disillusion began to set in as I watched peers gain global recognition for their music, while my career was sputtering along. I often felt as if my career was on a respirator waiting for someone to come along and pull the proverbial plug. Depression began to set in as I realized that the dream of stardom, fame, riches, and notoriety was escaping my grip. Although I had the perfect setup for success, everything promising seemed to be going nowhere, FAST!

One day while in the studio listening to vocals I had recently recorded, in my heart I asked God a question. Before I move further, let me qualify the previous statement. Growing up in church, I didn't know anything about the Scriptures, and I knew absolutely NOTHING about the Holy Spirit and prayer; however, I did have somewhat of a conviction that God was absolutely real! In fact, if I was driving down the street with music blasting in my car, I would turn the music completely down if I was approaching a church building.

Though I didn't know Him, I knew enough about Him to know He's holy, and that I should respect what belonged to Him, something that is all but evaporated in the generation of believers today (I digress). So, in my heart I asked God, "Why isn't my music taking off like I want it to?" To my surprise, I heard an answer that I'll never forget as long as I live! I don't know if I heard it with my natural ears, my head, or my heart. Nevertheless, I heard these words: "Because I've called you to Myself!" I was absolutely STUNNED! That divine interruption set off a series of events that completely changed the trajectory of my life and set my feet on a supernatural path I never knew existed. The fulcrum, however, was an actual DREAM!

In October 1997 I was living on Fort Meade Military Base in Maryland and was working two full-time jobs. I worked as a laborer through the night, and a store manager during normal hours. I was miserable. I was disillusioned. I was severely depressed. My music career that at one point was extremely promising had become completely stalled. While up north, I had supposed arrangements to work with world-famous artists, but those possibilities fell through.

I had become so dejected that I began to medicate emotionally with alcohol. I would work eight hours, from 10 p.m. to 6 a.m., and drink until it was time to leave for my next shift at 9 a.m. I was lonely and had no friends. Well…I had one friend; a guy who had recently served a prison sentence, and who was just as miserable as me. The old adage that misery loves company is absolutely true.

One morning after work, I went home and did what I would normally do every day after work, which was to soak my sorrows with hard liquor. I recall that morning so clearly. I drank myself to sleep. But what happened next would change my life forever!

While sleeping, I had a very vivid, Technicolor dream, in which I was back in my hometown at my grandmother's house. The colors in her home seemed more vibrant than in real life. In my dream, I was standing at the door of my grandmother's bedroom when she called out to me and asked me to walk with her to the other side of the house. As we walked together through the house, I noticed she was wearing a beautiful pink dress. There was no conversation or chatter; there was just the two of us walking together.

As we entered the living room, grandmother became faint and suddenly began to collapse. In a state of near panic, I took her into my arms and gently sat with her on the floor. As she lay in my arms, she proceeded to give me a message for our family. However, she began to be in agony as she struggled to convey what was on her heart, and in that way, she took her final breaths.

I awoke from the dream devastated! After all, I was my grandmother's favorite, and she was mine! I was so shaken by the dream; I began to weep uncontrollably. I immediately picked up the telephone and called her, but to my surprise, my mother answered the phone! "Mom," I said through tears and deep sobbing. "What's wrong, son?" she asked. "I just had a terrible dream! I dreamed that grandma passed away!"

I was crying so desperately. I had never had such a dream. Mom then asked, "Do you want to speak to your grandma?" Mom then gave the phone to Grandma, but she was in tremendous pain, so much so, that she couldn't even hold a conversation. "You

A SUDDEN INTERRUPTION

know, your grandmother has terminal cancer." I had NO IDEA.

You see, I was is such hot pursuit of becoming rich and famous, that I became far removed and disconnected from my family, so I was oblivious to her condition. Furthermore, I don't even know if I fully comprehended what terminal cancer was. I tell you, I was in a very bad state mentally and emotionally.

In the hours to follow, I shared the dream with my siblings, who scolded me for sharing such a dream, citing that I needed to be "positive." Nevertheless, exactly six days to the hour that I awoke from the dream, I received a phone call from a cousin, who informed me that my beautiful grandma had passed away.

Shortly after receiving the news, I came back to Florida for my grandmother's funeral. When I arrived, I immediately went to her house, where the entire family had gathered. As I sat in the driveway, my youngest sister came out to meet me. Shaken by the dream and the seemingly sudden death of Grandma, I dared not to go into the house, so my sister, Rachael, sat in the car and cried with me.

"How did it happen? How did she die?" I asked, fighting through tears. To my utter amazement, what Rachael described was EXACTLY what occurred in my dream! Grandma had asked my mother, who was Grandma's caregiver, to walk with her from her bedroom to the other side of the house. When they reached the living room, Grandma became faint, and breathed her last breath in my mother's arms! I was STUNNED!

The funeral was difficult, to say the least. I had decided sometime after the funeral that I would move back to Florida to be close to my family. Little did I know that the Lord had another plan, a sovereign plan at work that I knew nothing about. The truth was that God had begun a work in my heart.

> **I began to see that God was not a static, uninvolved relic of Baptist religion, but that at any moment He can superimpose realities of the eternal onto the temporal!**

He began showing me that, in however small a measure, there is a dimension of life that is vastly different than those things I had given myself to most of my life. I began to see that God was not a static, uninvolved relic of Baptist religion, but that at any moment He can superimpose realities of the eternal onto the temporal!

During the same time of my transition back home, a close friend from my hometown, Audrey, was going through a transformation of her own. She began to phone me, telling me about how she encountered God in such a profound way. As Audrey talked with me, she spoke of such things as the baptism of the Holy Spirit and encounters with God and the like—things that I was always intrigued about but had never heard mentioned by someone so young and with such passion and assurance!

On the one hand, my inward response was something like, "Wait a minute…this is AUDREY! And I know SHE isn't a Christian!" Yet, on the other hand, I knew Audrey, and this kind of talk wasn't normal for her. Something had happened to her! But I wasn't trying to hear too much of it. After all, I had my "reputation" to protect, and this Jesus stuff was the LAST thing I wanted to hear about.

You see, I had long decided that if I was going to do or be anything, I was going all the way! Hence, there wasn't room in my life for anything else. My purpose (so I thought) was to be a world star doing worldly things, and I wasn't about to compromise.

Looking back on that time in my life, I can more clearly see how God was pursuing me. Audrey was relentless in sharing her story whenever we talked, and after about four months of invitations to church, I agreed. The rest, as they say, is history!

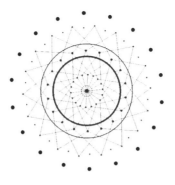

CHAPTER TWO

A TALE OF TWO KINGS

Before we venture any further, I want to tackle an important issue; that is, does God visit the unsaved in dreams? After all, in my experience of the dream foretelling my grandmother's death, I was not a Christian. Furthermore, everyone dreams (we'll discuss the scientific approach to dreams in a later chapter). So then, what made my dream a God-given dream? What's the proof?

I'm so glad you asked! Let's look at two men in the Bible who were both unsaved. Both were pagan kings and had no grid for how God speaks, much like how I was (except for the "king" part!). Let's look at Nebuchadnezzar and Pharaoh.

NEBUCHADNEZZAR

Daniel chapter 2 verse 1 gives a bit of insight into how the king was affected after having dreamed a dream in the night:

> "Now in the second year of the reign of Nebuchadnezzar, Nebuchadnezzar had dreams; and his spirit was troubled, and his sleep left him."[10]

To a certain degree, I understand acutely the disturbing feeling after having a dream. The psychological and sometimes physiological effects can leave a person restless and anxious, and even sometimes afraid. In fact, the dream encounter Nebuchadnezzar had was so overwhelming and traumatic that it even caused him to forget the details of the dream itself.

Shaken by what he had experienced, he called to himself all of the mystic specialists serving in his court to give him some consolation as to both what the dream was and what it meant. Yet none of them could offer any real help; they had absolutely nothing to work with.

---

[10] Dan 2:1, NASB

Nebuchadnezzar became furious at the impotent counsel of his magicians and threatened them with a morbid execution and the extermination of their families if they didn't immediately produce substantial answers. Of course, his demands were naturally unreasonable. However, the Most High God was at work behind the scenes. It was His intention that men would begin to grope for answers, in hopes that they would bump into Him! Job declared about the Lord,

> "With Him are wisdom and might;
> To Him belong counsel and understanding.
> "With Him are strength and sound wisdom,
> The misled and the misleader belong to Him.
> "He makes counselors walk barefoot
> and makes fools of judges."[11]

In other words, God alone has the absolute power to orchestrate the affairs of nations, and often He initiates conflict with the sole intention of making Himself known to mankind! That's AWESOME! What this means on an individual level is that the negative and often difficult situations that occur in our lives are actually opportunities for us to engage in seeking for God Himself in the midst of them.

---

[11] Job 12:13, 16-17, NASB

In the scenario with Nebuchadnezzar, his dream, forgetting about the dream, and subsequent failure of his wise men and magicians to produce answers was actually the activity of God setting the stage to put Himself on display.

The account goes on to describe how Daniel and his three friends went into prayer and worship and sought the face of God concerning the decree of the king to kill all the wise men, astrologers, and magicians. The text actually says that Daniel sought "mercies from the God of heaven concerning this *secret*."[12] To put it simply, Daniel and his friends understood there was a divine purpose with Jehovah to have concealed the dream and its meaning in such a fashion.

Job had a similar understanding relative to the mysteries of God and said, "He reveals mysteries *(secrets)* from the darkness and brings the deep darkness into light."[13] The One Who was responsible for *concealing* the secret was the only One able to *reveal* the secret.

After seeking God, Daniel and his friends received both the dream AND the divine interpretation of the dream. There were certain key results of having had the king's dream revealed and interpretation given: the lives of many were spared, the futures and destinies

---

[12] Dan 2:18, NKJV, emphasis mine
[13] Job 12:22, NASB

of nations were exposed, and the pagan king magnified the God of heaven! This is the response of King Nebuchadnezzar after Daniel told him both the dream and the interpretation:

> "Surely your God is a God of gods and a Lord of kings and a revealer of mysteries, since you have been able to reveal this mystery."[14]

God gave the dream to King Nebuchadnezzar in order to reveal Himself to the king, as well as to "make known to the king what shall come to pass."[15]

PHARAOH

Let's look at Pharaoh, king of Egypt, during the days of Joseph, the youngest son of Jacob. In those days, Egypt had become the superpower of the world. Joseph was the youngest of the twelve sons of Israel (Jacob), and was his father's darling son. He donned, as the Bible describes it, a coat of many colors made especially for him by his father and was therefore envied by his brothers when they saw that their father loved Joseph more than them.[16]

---

[14] Dan 2:47, NASB
[15] Dan 2:45, KJV
[16] Gen 37:4, NASB

During Joseph's childhood years, he often helped his older brothers in the field as they would feed their father's sheep. Along with the nepotism Joseph enjoyed as a teenager, he was also favored by God, as he received dreams on at least two occasions symbolizing God's intentions for his life, which included Joseph being raised to prominence above his brothers.

Although Joseph had these tremendous promises over his life, he suffered rejection from his older brothers, who despised him. In fact, it was when Joseph shared the dreams with his family that envy was incited in his brothers' hearts to the point that they would hatch a plan to kill him.

Can you imagine the power of his dreams? Can you imagine that the thoughts of God toward you and me are so powerful that, if we unscrupulously share them with the wrong people, it could literally cost us our very lives?

Oh, the marvelous thoughts God has toward you and me! I am thoroughly convinced if we would all get close enough to the Father, there would be no room in our hearts for envy or jealousy, for He would be able to make known to each of us the mystery of His will for our lives![17] Hallelujah!

---

[17] Eph 1:9, Ps 40:5, Jer 29:11, NASB

There must have been an element of worship, intimacy, and devotion to God in Joseph's personal life that influenced God to invade his dream life. "Why would you say a thing like that?" you might ask. Simply put, things don't just happen. There's always a cause-and-effect dynamic in spiritual realities in the lives of God's people.

> **Things don't just happen. There's always a cause-and-effect dynamic in spiritual realities in the lives of God's people.**

The closer we get to God in fasting, in prayer, in His Word, and in obedience, the more our lives become open to His dealings, His leadings, and His divine activity in our lives. The Scripture declares that if we draw near to God, He in turn will reciprocate that action![18] What a precious promise! Amen! Now back to our story.

So, Joseph receives dreams of grandeur and shares them with his older brothers, which incites them to hatch a plan to kill him and ditch his body in a pit. As they were planning the demise of Joseph, Reuben, the oldest of the pack, overhears them and talks them into sparing Joseph's life.

When Joseph arrived after being sent by his father to see what his brothers were up to and to give a report

---

[18] James 4:8, NASB

to him as to their work activities, his brothers seized him, stripped him of his coat of many colors, and threw him in an empty pit.

From there, a band of Ishmaelites purchased Joseph for twenty pieces of silver, and the Ishmaelites took him into Egypt. Joseph found himself as a slave in the estate of Potiphar, an officer of Pharaoh, king of Egypt, and was the commander of the king's guard.[19]

I don't know for certain, but surely any reasonable person can safely assume that Joseph experienced a fair amount of anxiety and fear as he had just been stripped of his homeland, ripped away from the loving relationship he shared with his father and mother, and taken against his will to a strange land of strange people and their strange gods. How did he survive? How did Joseph not lose his mind? How did Joseph not become bitter against his brothers? Against his God?

I firmly believe that an anchor in the storm raging in Joseph's soul was the dreams from God. I say this because though the circumstances were seemingly insurmountable, Joseph still thrived amid contradictory circumstances! Somehow, he could hold things together and find success wherever he found himself. Whether as a slave in Potiphar's estate or a prisoner in the penitentiary, the Bible says that Joseph prospered

---

[19] Gen 37:36, NASB

and that the Lord was with him. That implies Joseph's devotional life of prayer and intimacy with God was still intact.

How? After all he experienced, how is it that Joseph's heart was still alive with hope and expectation that God was for him and not against him? I believe it's because Joseph's dreams were not just dreaming; they were tantamount to THE VOICE OF GOD SPEAKING to him! It was the prophetic Word of the Lord!

Joseph reigned as a slave because in a dream the Word of the Lord to him was that he would reign! Joseph reigned in the prison because in a dream the Word of the Lord to him was that he would have dominion! The dream encounters Joseph experienced were as much a part of him than his very own name, and no circumstance or hardship posed a great enough threat to the dreams embedded in his heart and soul.

Joseph was tested by time, difficulty, hardships, false accusations, and prison, none of which were sufficient to shake him to the point that he abandoned what the Lord planted in his heart through the realm of his dream life.

Let me ask you a question: What is it that God has spoken concerning you? What dreams have you received from the Lord? It's time to redig the wells of your dreams and begin to ask God to reveal His will to you again! It's time to take up those forgotten dreams again and begin to walk in a revived faith, knowing that what God has shown you, He is more than able to bring to pass, irrespective of your current situation! Glory!

While Joseph was in prison, he encountered two men in the house of Pharaoh—a butler and a baker—who each had dreams that troubled them. Joseph gave them interpretations of their dreams, which ultimately catapulted him to the highest place in Pharaoh's palace, as second in command in all of Egypt, the most powerful nation on the planet in those days. What was the instrument God used to set Joseph in such an exalted place? Dreams!

Here's the story. While in prison, Joseph interpreted the dreams of Pharaoh's butler and baker. The baker met his demise at Pharaoh's hand, which was the interpretation of his dream. The butler was pardoned and restored back to his position in the palace, with the promise that, once reinstated, he would not forget Joseph. However, he forgot Joseph.

Imagine, Joseph remained in prison after having solved the riddle of the butler's dream, releasing the interpretation to him, and seeing him restored back to the palace in full expectation of his own restoration… but the butler failed to return the favor!

However, after two years of being forgotten, something amazing happened! Something supernatural took place! Pharaoh dreamed! In fact, he dreamed twice, and his dreams disturbed his spirit so much that he, like we observed with Nebuchadnezzar, called for the magicians and wise men to help him; yet none of his diviners could give an interpretation! Suddenly, Mr. Butler remembered the Hebrew youth from the prison house! Here's his account:

> "Pharaoh was furious with his servants, and he put me in confinement in the house of the captain of the bodyguard, *both* me and the chief baker. We had a dream on the same night, he and I; each of us dreamed according to the interpretation of his *own* dream. Now a Hebrew youth *was* with us there, a servant of the captain of the bodyguard, and we related *them* to him, and he interpreted our dreams for us. To each one he interpreted according to his *own* dream. And just as he interpreted for us, so it happened; he restored me in my office, but he hanged him."[20]

The butler's testimony of his encounter with Joseph opened an immediate door for Joseph to stand before Pharaoh to interpret his dreams, and to counsel

---

20 Gen 41:10-13, NASB

him concerning how to respond to what Jehovah was saying concerning future events. This ultimately catapulted Joseph to be the most influential person on the entire planet—with the exception of Pharaoh himself. In fact, here's how Pharaoh responds to Joseph's dream interpretation and corresponding wisdom:

> "Moreover, Pharaoh said to Joseph, 'Though I am Pharaoh, yet without your permission no one shall raise his hand or foot in all the land of Egypt.' Then Pharaoh named Joseph Zaphenath-paneah."[21]

What a staggering statement! What an august promotion of responsibility! The name "Zaphenath-paneah" literally means "prince or ruler of the life of this age"! In other words, through the spiritual endowment of dreams and interpretations, God elevated Joseph to be the ruler of the age in which he lived. What Joseph's father Jacob became in "name," Joseph became in "function." Typically, this is to be the function and calling of the true Church of Jesus in the earth today!

God has ordained through an endowment of power of the Spirit and the exercising of spiritual gifts that

---

[21] Gen 41:44-45, NASB

His Church governs the affairs of this life, reigning in this life by Him. It is the baptism in the Holy Ghost that provides to the Church the divine equipment to accomplish such supernatural feats as these.

The POWER that was guaranteed to the disciples of Jesus as they waited in the Upper Room contained within it the enablement to dream dreams and see visions (more on that later).[22] It's also important to note that what Pharaoh saw in his dreams was not simply the course of nature; it was in fact a revealing of "what He (God) is about to do."[23] It was the unveiling of God's secret, and how He was to judge the entire earth with famine, as well as the merciful plan in the Wisdom of God to sustain life—to the glory of His Own Name—through His servants in the earth.

---

[22] Joel 2:28, Acts 2:17, NASB
[23] Gen 41:25, NKJV

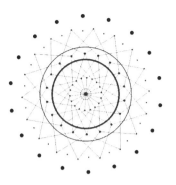

CHAPTER THREE

WAYS IN WHICH GOD SPEAKS

From the beginning of creation, the Father has communicated with humanity. However, not all of God's communication is the same with each person with which He speaks. For example, in the book of Numbers there is an altercation between Moses and his siblings, Miriam and Aaron. The Lord comes down in a cloud and calls a meeting between Himself and the three siblings to mediate the situation, and it is in this context that He provides intel for at least two ways that He speaks to mankind. The account in the book of Numbers reads as follows:

"If there is a prophet among you,
I, the Lord, shall make Myself known to him ***in a vision***.
I shall speak with him ***in a dream***.
"Not so, with My servant Moses,
He is faithful in all My household;
With him I speak ***mouth to mouth***,
Even ***openly***, and not in dark sayings,
And he beholds the form of the Lord."[24]

One thing of note here is how the Lord draws clear distinction between the ways in which He speaks to individuals. First, there is not a uniformed method of communication when God chooses to reveal Himself or His counsel to us. Second, as seen in the verse above, He, intentionality and specificity, juxtaposed His communication of choice to prophets and to those He handpicks for a specific function. As for the prophet, the Lord makes Himself, His will, counsel, Person etc., known in what seems to be two common or generic ways: 1) He discloses things concerning Himself "***in a vision***."[25] 2) He reveals Himself "***in a dream***." Let us spend a moment discussing the nature and importance of visions.

---

[24] Num 12:6-8, NASB, emphasis mine
[25] Num 12:6, NASB

The Hebrew root for our English word rendered "vision" is "mar'ah," which is elsewhere translated "looking glass," which suggests the ability to see or behold as by peering into something reflective. We see mar'ah used as looking glass in Exodus 38 during the construction of the Tabernacle and its furnishings. Verse 8 says, "They made the bronze basin and its bronze stand from **the mirrors** of the women who served at the entrance to the tent of meeting."[26]

The brass basin, or brazen laver, as the King James Version renders, was the first place of encounter in the Tabernacle of Moses, where the priest would ceremonially wash as he peered into the mirror of the basin. This is a picture of our interaction with the Word of God. The Word of the Lord is like a mirror, exposing flaws of human flesh, the true condition of the human heart, and revealing the contrasting beauty and perfection of the Lord and the burning passion of His heart for humanity.

Proverbs chapter 27 verse 19 says, "As in water face reflects face, So the heart of man reflects man."[27] In this verse, there are two profound dynamics (among many others) to be discovered here. The first is the use of water as a "mirror reflecting the face." First, the water of the Word gives us great clarity for our lives, as

---

[26] Ex 38:8, NIV
[27] Prov 27:19, NASB

it washes away the crud that impedes our view of Who Jesus is.

Second, just as the bronze basin was filled with water and used to wash the hands and face of the priest, so the Word washes and cleanses us at the heart level, so that the fruit of our lives begins to reflect the will of God in and through us more perfectly as we encounter Him.

As we peer into the mirror of God's Word, we receive revelation by the Spirit of the person and glory of God.

The New Testament says in 2 Corinthians chapter 3 verse 18 that we as Christians "behold as in a mirror the glory of the Lord, are being transformed into the same image."[28] As we peer into the mirror of God's Word, we receive revelation by the Spirit of the person and glory of God, which gives us clarity and transforms our ways and gives our lives direction and meaning, causing us to be carriers of His glory in the earth. So, for the prophet to whom God's speaks, the foundation of divine interaction is the Scriptures, as God said to Aaron and Miriam. The prophetic spirit must be, therefore, both activated and cultivated in the mirror of the Bible.

---

[28] 2 Cor 3:18, NASB

The Lord continues to explain His methods of revelation. He says, "and I will speak to them in dreams." In the original language, the word for "dreams' is the Hebrew word "chalowm" or "chalam," which in this context means "to receive intel or communication while in a state of dumbness." In this way, our natural or physical faculties are suspended, and our subconscious receives images, ideas, sensations, and even emotions.

In a state of sleep or unconsciousness, the Spirit of God can transmit information to us, through dreams, while bypassing the defenses of our conscious self that would naturally object or resist new intel that might be in conflict with any prior knowledge, established structures, or systems of belief that may exist within.

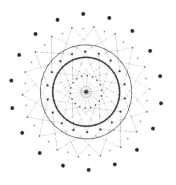

CHAPTER FOUR

DREAMS AND REVELATION

It's remarkable that God initiates communication with man, and that He often uses the method of dreams to articulate His mind to mere human beings. In fact, it is an expression of the mercy of God to extend Himself to us, breaking through to us in our striving and hardheartedness after having spoken to us by voice or by His Word. This is frequently the condition of the human heart when the Father sends dreams to us in the night. Consider the following statements written in the book of Job:

> "Why do you accuse God of never answering?
> "Although God speaks again and again,
> no one pays attention to what he says."[29]

It is of note that Elihu, one of Job's witnesses to his suffering, makes an important observation about the ways in which God communicates to man, as well as our tendency to not only misconceive when He is speaking, but also to be oblivious to the voice of the Lord altogether.

There are often a multitude of reasons for why we are predisposed to not perceiving God's many attempts to speak to us. Sin, the flesh, distractions, busyness, and ignorance are just a few of a thousand reasons we can miss God. Yet, in the merciful kindness of God, He often waits until our human weakness is subdued and our faculties are suspended, and suddenly breaks through to the subconscious with dreams in the night, delivering to us the divine instructions we so desperately need! Praise God! Elihu explains how and why God speaks to us in this way:

> "At night when people are asleep, God speaks in dreams and visions. He makes them listen to what he says."[30]

---

[29] Job 15:13-14, GNT
[30] Job 33:15-16, GNT

Our human functions are literally bypassed, giving way to God's good Word to us in an attempt to deliver us from our hang-ups, bringing us ever closer to His desire for our lives, which is always good! Because we are frail and prone to wander into sinful and destructive patterns, the Father so graciously and passionately pursues us with every intention of breaking us out of strongholds and setting our feet back onto the foundations of righteous paths He's foreordained.

> "He makes them listen to what he says, and <u>they are frightened at his warnings</u>. God speaks <u>to make them stop their sinning</u> and to save them."[31]

The Father understands perfectly that not all of us are particularly spiritually mature, and, as a good parent, He insulates us as much as necessary, protecting us so that we are not eternally injured on the journey to becoming mature sons and daughters of God. There are several examples in the New Testament of how God breaks through our immaturity and limited understanding of His divine will and sends us instructions through dreams and visions. We will explore and

---

[31] Job 33:16-17, GNT, emphasis added

unpack important points in the book of Job relative to dreams in later chapters.

The very beginnings of the life of our Lord in the earth was marked by angelic visitations and supernatural dreams. In fact, there were five times in the early life of our Lord where His earthly parents were either led specifically by the Word of the Lord through dreams or were significantly impacted by the revelation of and obedience to dreams of others. Let us consider a few major successive events recorded in the gospel of Matthew, which provide for us a window into the interactions between the invisible and visible realms through dream activity.

JOSEPH, HUSBAND TO MARY, MOTHER OF OUR LORD

One such example is with Joseph, husband to Mary, the mother of our Lord. When news came of his young fiancée's pregnancy, Joseph was greatly distressed and disturbed—and rightly so! Being the righteous man that he was, his intention was to honor God, even in the midst of what seemed to be a scandalous situation of adultery that led to an unwed pregnancy. Consider the text:

"Joseph, her fiancé, was a good man and did not want to disgrace her publicly, so he decided to break the engagement quietly. As he considered this, **an angel of the Lord appeared to him in a dream.**"[32]

Joseph was in an ostensibly bad situation, which would have warranted the legal and justifiable divorce. His fiancée was pregnant, and Joseph knew for a *fact* he was not the father! That, my friends, is a MAJOR issue!

Imagine you were well established in the community as a person of integrity and impeccable character, and one who was a model of fidelity to the emerging generation. You are engaged to marry a beautiful young damsel, who, as far as you know, is sexually pure and has never had a reputation for impropriety or scandal.

Over the course of time, your courtship transitions to betrothal, and you begin counting down the days to consummation. Everything is made ready; you invite all of your family and friends to the wedding ceremony, and just before the wedding day, your fiancée—the one you presumed was pure and undefiled—drops a news bomb of reality TV proportion! I'M PREGNANT!

---

[32] Matt 1:19-20, NLT, emphasis added

Can you imagine the shock? Can you picture the pain of emotion and mental distress Joseph experienced?

Yet, in all of the swirl of reasons he might have had to pull the plug on the engagement and out Mary as a cheating, no good, dirty so-and-so, he decides to withhold adjudication, and sleep on the matter! And, thank God, he did!

The same night, as Joseph pondered the ramifications of the situation and the weight of the decisions he was faced with, **he has a dream**! Oh, the faithfulness of God to break through the fog of uncertainty in Joseph's heart and mind and bring clarity that would illuminate the annals of both time and eternity with a dream! Here's the account:

> "An angel of the Lord appeared to him **in a dream**. 'Joseph, son of David,' the angel said, 'do not be afraid to take Mary as your wife. For the child within her was conceived by the Holy Spirit.' All of this occurred to fulfill the Lord's message through his prophet: 'Look! The virgin will conceive a child! She will give birth to a son, and they will call him Immanuel, which means "God is with us." ' "[33]

---
[33] Matt 1:20, 22-23, NLT

DREAMS AND REVELATION

It's wonderful to know that, despite Joseph's inward turmoil of uncertainty, God didn't leave him in that state. I would also argue the probability that because of the psychological and emotional crisis Joseph was experiencing at the news of his fiancée's untimely pregnancy, he was not in a place to hear from the Lord.

How many times in my life have I been so enamored with the cares of life and the shock of unforeseen circumstances, that I became mentally, emotionally, and physically consumed? While in such a condition, the absence of the presence of peace makes it nearly impossible to even think rationally, let alone hear the voice of God!

> **We are human, and because of our fallenness, we bear the residual effects of brokenness and frailty.**

We are human, and because of our fallenness, we bear the residual effects of brokenness and frailty. However, King David said that God "knoweth our frame; He remembereth that we are **DUST**."[34] Because God is ever mindful of our human frailty and weakness, He extends Himself to us in His kindness, going the extra mile to give us the instructions we need to live successfully in the earth. King David goes on to

---

[34] Ps 103:14, KJV

say of God, "As a father shows compassion to his children, so the LORD shows compassion to those who fear him."[35]

In Joseph's moment of distress in what seemed to be an insurmountable situation, God broke through the veil of his weakness with a dream, which ultimately set the course of his life and the earthly life of our Lord for the next thirty-three-and-a-half years! This truth can be a great encouragement to sincere American Christians because, though we are often beset and distracted by the trappings of prosperity and entertainment, God knows just how to break through our dullness and reignite fresh vision and purpose to a sleeping Church through the release of dreams and visions!

Let us be intentional in asking God for and expecting more dream activity from the realm of eternity!

Let us be intentional in asking God for and expecting more dream activity from the realm of eternity! Let us pray in faith, believing that the One who earnestly sees and hears our prayers desires to give us the things we ask for! Beloved, the Lord of heaven and earth LOVES to interact with His children, and He is waiting to be accosted in the arena of faith in order

---

[35] Ps 103:13, ESV

that His divine will is laid hold of and manifested in the visible realm. Hallelujah!

THE MAGI'S JOURNEY

One of the most popular aspects of the Christmas drama is that of the visit of the wise men (Magi) from the East to Jerusalem. There is great mystery and intrigue surrounding this historical account, as there very well should be, for at least two reasons: 1) these three Magi, obviously non-Jewish persons, traveled for probably two years after observing the appearance of a sign in the heavens. On their two-year journey they caravanned with their treasuries of enormous amounts of wealth and commodities for one specific purpose: to *worship the King of the Jews*![36] 2) Given the fact these men were not of Hebrew or Jewish origin and not from Jerusalem, *how* did they know the significance of the "star" they followed? In fact, *why* would they even know what this star signified? Let us consider a very logical and probable explanation.

---

[36] Matt 2:2, NASB

ISRAEL'S NOTORIETY AND POPULARITY

The nation of Israel was widely known and greatly honored among the nations of the earth for their prevailing knowledge and practice of science. However, the particular aspects of the sciences they specialized in were not the normative mainstream genres of science today. Instead of chemistry, geology, astronomy, mathematics, conventional engineering, etc., the science of the Hebrews extended chiefly into music, architecture, natural history, agriculture, morals, theology, war, and *the knowledge of future events*![37] Furthermore, there are numerous accounts in the Scriptures detailing the direct involvement of the God of Israel with His people, providing supernatural intelligence in order to ensure Israel's success in the earth in each of the above-mentioned areas.

In several of these accounts, news of the victories secured by the people of the Lord would quickly spread throughout the nations of the earth, and both their enemies and allies alike would seek to know the secrets to their successes.

While we can enumerate multiple examples, one important occasion is Babylon's siege and capture of Jerusalem, the capital city of Israel, in 607 BC during

---

[37] "Barnes Notes: Daniel," *Bible Hub*, https://biblehub.com/commentaries/barnes/daniel/1.htm.

the time of Daniel the prophet. During the acquisition, Nebuchadnezzar, king of Babylon, issued a command to apprehend certain of the children of Israel, particularly those who, among other things, were "cunning in knowledge, and understanding science."[38]

Daniel and his three friends, Azariah, Mishael, and Hananiah, who were among the youth selected with such qualifications, were eventually found to be "ten times better" than all the magicians and astrologers (wise men) in the whole of the kingdom of Babylon. These four young men are characterized as having been given by God "knowledge and skill in ALL learning and wisdom." Specifically, however, Daniel is uniquely endowed with "understanding in ALL visions and dreams."[39]

> **Visions and dreams were primary means by which the Most High God would unfold future events to the prophets, especially in Old Testament Scriptures.**

It is of note that visions and dreams were primary means by which the Most High God would unfold future events to the prophets, especially in Old Testament Scriptures. Often, individuals would have visions filled with symbols and signs, but were unable

---

[38] Dan 1:3-4, NASB
[39] Dan 1:17, KJV

to "decode" the vision or dream in order to ascertain its meaning. Many throughout the history of the nation of Israel were skillful dream and visionary interpreters and had consequently gained a reputation for accurately predicting future events, warranting the land of Israel to become known as "the land of the prophets."

It's also important to remember that these Hebrew youths were deported from their native land of Judah and were carried away as captives into the Far East land of Babylon, where they were obliged to the service of the king. It is, therefore, not far-fetched to assume that Daniel, even as a young man, was given the task of teaching and instructing the magicians and astrologers in the court of the king in his areas of gifting relative to visions and dreams, especially since he was regarded as being "ten times better" than all others in the whole realm of Babylon.[40]

Eventually, this supernatural endowment in Daniel's life elevated him to high prominence, as he was the lone official with the ability to both reveal and interpret the king's dream, which caused his renown to transcend the many regime changes in Babylon, as well as the overthrow of the Babylonian kingdom by the Medes and Persians.

---

[40] Dan 1:20, KJV

It is from this Medo-Persian dominated land in the East that the Magi would originate, making their two-year journey to Jerusalem, seeking to worship the King of the Jews. That they would have been instructed in the ways of Daniel, and therefore would have had understanding in the Hebrew sciences of prophecy (the knowledge of future events), the realm of dreams, and dream interpretation is certainly plausible.

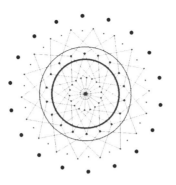

CHAPTER FIVE

DREAMS, INTERPRETATION, AND PROPHECY

There are *MANY* things of resources, both natural and supernatural, and things of provision, that the Lord has stored up for the success and prosperity of His people in the earth. However, in order to apprehend and access those hidden things, the people of God must be rightly positioned. The Lord has chosen to hide many things IN HIM in the realm of the Spirit in order that sons and daughters of God are the only ones to rightfully and legally possess them.

Paul the apostle declares in 1 Corinthians chapter 2 verse 7, "But we speak the wisdom of God in a *mystery*, *even* the *hidden wisdom*, which God ordained before the world *unto our glory.*"[41] The apostle said there are mysterious things over in the realm of the eternal that God has purposed for us to benefit from both now and in eternity. The very fact that He has ordained or "set things up" to be this way should give us confidence in our pursuit of Him, knowing that there are rewards in store, and these rewards are for both for the glory of God and for the glorification of the Church! To be *"glorified"* literally means to be *"honorable, praiseworthy, and dignified."*

For far too long, the Western Church has fallen into some sort of stupor, resting on past accomplishments and what prior momentum has afforded, and has forfeited her right to access current resources available to her in the realm of the Spirit. We have become spoiled. We have become indifferent. We have adopted an "insta" mentality given to us by the world's system where gratification is immediate. However, there is a work, a labor to be employed if we are to live supernaturally, and if we are to lay hold of those glorious things the Lord has prepared for our glorification and success in Him.

Even the realm of dreams possesses hidden things which must be searched out and interpreted in order to

---

[41] 1 Cor 2:7, KJV

receive their benefits and for lives to be gloriously enriched by them. Dreams are a dialect of the Last Days language of God to and through His Church. If this is true, there must also (and dare I say, EQUALLY) be the ability in the Church to interpret the language of dreams. Consider what the apostle Paul says concerning spiritual language in 1 Corinthians chapter 14 verse 13: "Therefore, the one who speaks in a *language* should pray that he may interpret."

If we speak the language of dreams in the Last Days, we should equally possess the ability to translate dreams by the grace of God.

So then, if we speak the language of dreams in the Last Days, we should equally possess the ability to translate dreams by the grace of God. Dreams in the night are often signs pointing to a greater reality. Yet, these signs often need to be interpreted if they are to serve a purpose; otherwise they are experiences at best.

It's important to understand that English is not the standard language of heaven; neither is Spanish, French, Greek, or Hebrew. Rather, the standard language of heaven is God Himself through the Eternal Spirit. Even in the earth, when God speaks, His words, thoughts, emotions, and actions must be translated or interpreted in order that the soul of man understands and comprehends. Thus, tongues and interpretation of tongues can be understood in part in this way: unknown tongues are the language of God through or by the Spirit; interpretation of tongues is the translation of spiritual language into that which can be understood, hence for the edifying of the human hearer.

In theory, this sequence of understanding can be clearly observed in the book of Acts chapter 2 verses 4 to 6, which reads as such: "And they were all filled with the Holy Ghost, and began to speak with other tongues, as *the Spirit gave them utterance*. And there were dwelling at Jerusalem Jews, devout men, out of every nation under heaven. Now when this was noised abroad, *the multitude came together, and were confounded*, because that *every man heard them speak in his own language*."

Notice the pattern:

1. The Spirit inspires expression of heaven's language.
2. There were others in proximity of the Holy Spirit's activity, but were not of similar origin or geographic location.
3. Vicinity to both understand and be edified.

Another example can be found in the apostle Paul's initial letter to the church at Corinth. In it, he commends the church for their unfettered flowing of spiritual gifts when they came together corporately. The apostle then begins to advise as to how they could have maximum impact and edification by explaining the implications of what could happen if there was spiritual expression without translation or interpretation.

In 1 Corinthians chapter 14 verses 23 to 25, the apostle Paul explains a scenario where the church is gathered for worship and is under the unction and utterance of the Holy Spirit. If the church, he says, is engaged only in "speaking with (heavenly) tongues, and there come in *those that are* unlearned, or unbelievers, will they not say that ye are mad?"[42] In other words, even though the Spirit is clearly moving through the church, both the spiritually immature and unbelieving ones will be completely unbenefited, because there is no bridge to understanding what the Holy Spirit is saying and doing.

Conversely, the apostle goes on to explain the impact of a gathering in which there is both the expression of the language of the Spirit AND the unveiling or interpretation of that language in the presence of the unlearned and unbelieving; "*he is convinced* (convicted

---

[42] 1 Cor 14:23-25, NASB

in his heart) of all, *he is judged* of all (weighs both the motives and intentions of his heart before God): And thus are *the secrets of his heart made manifest*; and so falling down on *his* face *he will worship God*."[43]

Just as in the scenario in the book of Acts chapter 2 verses 4 to 41 where about three thousand people repented of their sins, received salvation, and were added to the Church, the unlearned and unbeliever alike were provided a bridge of translation, moving them from immaturity and unbelief into a life of worship of the one true God!

The ability to perceive and receive the language of God at the heart level enables us to address crippling things in our hearts that would otherwise go unnoticed.

The ability to perceive and receive the language of God at the heart level enables us to address crippling things in our hearts that would otherwise go unnoticed, and to make the necessary changes so that we can be useful to God and beneficial to those around us. Some might ask, "Why does God need to speak in code? Why is He so mysterious and difficult to understand?"

---

[43] 1 Cor 14:24-25, NASB, emphasis added

Here is an absolute fact: Whenever there has been a communication gap between God and man, the fault has without fail been with us and not God! Actually, the Godhead is the same today as yesterday, and even billions of years prior if He could be measured in time. He has not changed. In fact, according to the Bible, God CANNOT change. But WE have changed. Humanity is fallen. And, because humanity is fallen, we must be born of God and enter into a process of maturation until we can think, act, and live like the God Who created us in His image.

God is not mysterious for mystery's sake, nor does He delight in being difficult and hard to understand. Rather, He is mysterious and often misunderstood because of the fallenness of the ones who once existed in perfection, having been created in the mirror image of the Creator Himself.

Before the fall in Eden, mankind existed in utter perfection, having no deficits in our ability to know, understand, perceive, and fully comprehend God. This is evidenced, in part, by Adam's instant ability to fully walk in his role as administrator and principal steward of the inhabited earth.

Genesis chapter 2 verse 19 explains how, after having commissioned Adam to have dominion and authority over the earth, God brings every bird of the air and beast of the field to Adam to see what *he* would call them.[44] Obviously, Adam underwent no maturation process in order to qualify him to have ruling influence over the earth in such a way. It's also important to remember that neither Adam nor Eve was born into the earth. They were both created—Adam from the dust of the earth, and Eve from the side of Adam—as fully mature humans covered only in the glory of God which never paled, and neither were they spiritually dry.

Adam and Eve lived exclusively by the Spirit, and consequently all of their spiritual faculties were in perfectly good working order. Their disobedience, however, proved to be an eternally fatal error, causing them to descend into the throws of death in the worst ways, and chief among them was their ability to perceive themselves and God accurately.

For in Genesis chapter 3 verse 10, Adam, responding to the voice of the Lord God calling to him, reveals his spiritual condition by saying when he heard God's voice, he was afraid because he was naked, and he hid himself.[45] This condition of his was in stark contrast to his state of existence in Genesis chapter 2 verse 25, stating they were both "naked and unashamed."

---

[44] Gen 2:19, NASB
[45] Gen 3:10, NASB

According to Strong's Exhaustive Concordance of the Bible, the Hebrew word translated "naked and unashamed" is "buwsh" (pronounced 'boo-sha'), which means to be radiant; not pale; to be completely oriented with regard to one's sense of time, place, identity, or purpose; it also implies crispness, liveliness, intellectual or physiological sharpness, etc.

Therefore, when Adam sinned, all of the above-mentioned attributes he possessed were instantly corrupted, impeding his ability to perceive God accurately as he did before the fall. The awesome news is, our wonderful Lord Jesus Christ, when He was sent into the world, gave power to all those who receive Him to become the sons of God, even as Adam before the fall, being born of God anew![46] Praise His glorious Name forevermore!

When Jesus ascended forty days after the resurrection, He sent to all who believe and are saved the promised Holy Spirit, who is to lead us into ALL TRUTH! Beloved ones, this is precisely the means by which we are enabled to accurately perceive God and the mysterious things of God. It is only by the Spirit that we are able to comprehend "the mysterious and hidden wisdom of God, which He destined <u>for our glory</u> before time began!"[47]

---

[46] John 1:12-13, NASB
[47] 1 Cor 2:7, BSB

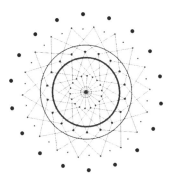

CHAPTER SIX

THE JOURNEY INTO REVELATION

The desire of God's heart to be in continuous communion and communication with His sons and daughters cannot be overstated. In fact, King David said of the Lord, that He "humbles Himself to behold the things that are in heaven and in the earth."[48] Other versions of the same verse say, He "stoops down" in order that He might interact with the things in heaven and earth. What manner of God is this, Who, though the heavens cannot contain Him in all of His glory,

---

[48] Ps 113:6, NASB

extends Himself to the degree that makes it possible for the finite to touch the Infinite?

Even from the beginning, it was the Living God Who took up the dust of the earth into His hands and breathed into it the breath of Life! The Mighty God, the Self-existent God Who exists outside of the realm of time, which He Himself created, somehow steps into time for the sole purpose of making Himself known to man who is made in His image and likeness!

The psalmist goes on to explain the purpose of this unfathomable act of humility: "He raises up the poor from the dust and lifts the needy out of the ash heap; To make them sit with princes, With the princes of His people."[49]

The God of all creation humbles Himself for our glorification, as the great apostle Paul tells us in 1 Corinthians chapter 2 verse 7! It is with this same desire, I believe, that God releases dreams with hidden meanings. It's not only the message that is of critical importance, but also the process of searching out the meaning of the dream that has massive benefits to the heart of man.

When we pursue the Pursuer of humanity, transformation begins to happen within the heart and eventually metamorphosis takes place in the soul. As we

---

[49] Ps 113:7-8, NASB

begin to seek God with questions concerning what He is communicating to us, we enter into a sort of divine transaction, which brings purification and transformation to the soul.

The limitations and frailties of our flesh become dim in comparison to the increase of the brightness of the glory in our inner man. As our hearts turn towards Jesus, Who is the Truth, the veil of dullness is removed. We can then behold Him in all of His glory and are thereby transformed into His image.[50]

King Solomon alludes to such a process, where he speaks of the pursuit of hidden and mysterious things as being honorable and glorious.[51] What brings honor and glory is not the pursuit in and of itself; rather, it is how the process of discovery profoundly impacts the heart of the pursuer. As God extends Himself to humanity through dreams, the response and inclination of the heart, the mind, and the desire of the soul touching

> **As our hearts turn towards Jesus, Who is the Truth, the veil of dullness is removed. We can then behold Him in all of His glory and are thereby transformed into His image.**

---

[50] 2 Cor 3:14-18, NASB
[51] Prov 25:2, NASB

the eternal and infinite God bring purification and unrivalled satisfaction.

King Solomon qualifies the attained glory of the pursuit in the ensuing verses: "Take away the dross (impurities) from the silver, and the smith has material for a vessel; take away the wicked from the presence of the king, and his throne will be established in righteousness."[52] In other words, as the pursuit of the hidden things of God ensues, God brings cleansing and purification to the heart of the pursuer, which produces righteousness and makes one useful for the benefit of his or her society.

When we become captivated by what the Lord gives us a window into, we inevitably encounter the cleansing fire of God.

When we become captivated by what the Lord gives us a window into, we inevitably encounter the cleansing fire of God. It is no coincidence that King Solomon, who was commissioned by his father, David, to build the Lord's house, encountered the fire of heaven after he began to seek out the revelation of God to Moses, which was hidden in the mountains at Gibeon. Though the Ark of the Covenant was gone,

---

[52] Prov 25:4-5, NASB

it was actually not the object of Solomon's pursuit; he was actually seeking the Brazen Altar.[53]

What's even more awe-inspiring is the fact that God was pursuing Solomon at the same time! The Lord made Himself personally known to Solomon in Gibeon through a dream in the night. One night at Gibeon the Lord appeared to Solomon in a dream, and God said, "Ask, and I will give it to you!" What a holy visitation! What a divine invitation from the Lord, to have an open check (so to speak) given through a dream as a reward of pursuit!

It pleases God very much when His children possess the faith to shrug off the flesh and the many distractions and cares of life and set their heart on the pilgrimage of pursuit! He is certainly a rewarder of them that diligently seek Him, and His ultimate reward is Himself! The fact that the Lord's visit to Solomon was through a dream is massively implicative on many levels!

First, Solomon had recently given a mammoth offering to the Lord at the altar of sacrifice. The Lord could have chosen to bear witness to the sacrifice with fire and glory as He did in the ensuing chapters! However, God showed Himself in a dream, and when

---

[53] 2 Chron 1:5, NASB

a dream is given of God, it indelibly writes upon the heart!

Second, God used a dream to inaugurate and establish the foundation of Solomon's reign as king of Israel and Judah. Again, external and ceremonial pageantry benefitted the people, but the dream given by the Lord to young and tender Solomon was the ineradicable mark on his heart that would be with him the rest of his days on the earth. Even after his blatant disobedience and the consequence of losing the kingdom, Solomon could rest in the hope of the mercy of the Lord because of what was written on his heart through a dream!

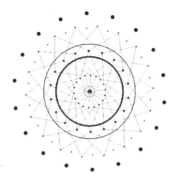

CHAPTER SEVEN

DIVINE UNDERSTANDING: THE KEY TO DISCERNING DREAMS

Once in a dream, I was in a context where I was surrounded by academics in a seminary school. While sitting in the midst of academics, one after the other began to heave criticisms and accusations concerning things of the Bible that I had apparently preached and wrote. Suddenly, the Spirit of God came upon me and I began to answer my critics. I said by the Spirit to one of the accusers, "You have all of this Bible knowledge from which you hurl accusations, but you have no understanding. Knowledge comes from study, but understanding comes from God!"

As I proclaimed that statement under the function of the Holy Spirit, I noticed that the words on the pages of their Bibles disappeared, and the pages were turned into clear, plastic sheets. In the dream, I knew the Lord was speaking to me personally concerning the difference between the acquisition of knowledge and divine understanding.

I had recently started to pursue a master's in divinity, and I had concerns that the instructors and several students were much smarter than I, but I also had grave disagreements with many of the things that were said in the classroom context. It was difficult for me to respond to a topic of discussion or write a paper without being quizzical of some of the key points and statements they expressed. This was cause for me to feel a bit insecure, because my knowledge of philosophy and the great thinkers of the past was limited. However, through this dream, the Spirit of God gave me a key to overcome the adversities of academia and its esoteric nature.

The possession of divine understanding is critical in the establishing of someone in all of life, and especially in things pertaining to God and His purposes in the earth. It is King Solomon who exclaimed the importance of understanding when he said to "incline

DIVINE UNDERSTANDING: THE KEY TO DISCERNING DREAMS

thine ear unto wisdom and apply thine heart to understanding."[54] Notice that understanding doesn't necessarily come by the consumption of information through books—devouring teachings from your favorite teacher, sage, guru, or rabbi. Rather, there must be employment of the heart before there can be the acquisition of understanding.

The question must be begged, however, what does practically applying your heart look like? Solomon qualifies applying the heart with the following statement: "*If you cry out* for insight and *lift up your voice* for understanding."[55] So then, the application of the heart in the pursuit of attaining understanding from God is embodied through the lifting up of the voice in cries to God in the place of prayer!

This way of praying is elsewhere described as supplication, which is passionate, voluminous prayer; prayer with fervency and intensity. By definition, supplication is the antithesis of the kind of prayer expressed when thanksgiving is offered for something you already possess, such as when one prays before a meal.

Supplication is loud, obnoxious, and often embarrassing when expressed in the company of others. Nevertheless, it is the key necessity for obtaining divine understanding. Thusly, Solomon says that only after

---

[54] Prov 2:2
[55] Prov 2:3, AMP

this kind of prayer, this kind of passionate crying out is released from a desperate and empty heart, can one be filled with an endowment of living understanding from God.

Let us expound upon things pertaining to Solomon mentioned earlier in the book. As stated, it was in this profound spirit of the pursuit of the knowledge and understanding of God that King Solomon sought the Lord during his transition from being prince of David to king of Israel. Solomon knew he was at a great disadvantage because of his youth and inexperience, and that he needed something of divine proportion in order to successfully lead God's flock, the people of Israel. What's interesting is the fact of Solomon's choosing to not seek the face of God in Jerusalem, where the ark of God resided. Rather, he journeyed to Gibeon of all places.

Supplication is the key necessity for obtaining divine understanding.

Why Gibeon? Because it was the location of the altar of sacrifice. It was the high place. It is fascinating that, while all Israel relished in the idea of having the ark of God among them in Jerusalem, and boasted in confidence of the strength, might, and protection of God in their midst by way of the ark, Solomon forsook the ark in pursuit of the ALTAR! Even so it is in our day.

There are MANY who seek to exalt the worship of the ark of the presence of God, and in so doing, forsake the altar of sacrifice, which is the prerequisite for true presence and glory! Would to God we would return to the divine order of things in our day! Notwithstanding, "the king went to Gibeon to sacrifice there; for that was the great high place: a thousand burnt offerings did Solomon offer upon that altar."[56]

It's important to note that the "burnt offerings" Solomon offered was not for his sins; the burnt offering represents the offering of oneself to God. It was a symbol of the nature of man (typified by the bull and its stubborn, untamable, and destructive nature) being put to death and consumed by the fire of God in exchange for the nature of God. And Solomon offered a THOUSAND of them, as if to say "Lord, I die a thousand deaths to my own corrupt nature in exchange for Your nature to live in me."

As such, the thousand burnt offerings represented the intense cry of Solomon's heart. In fact, it was precisely this heart cry the Lord responds to, as He appears to Solomon by night in his dream. The Lord specifically identifies the reason for His visitation to Solomon, saying, "because this (the passionate cries

---

[56] 1 Kings 3:4

and desire for divine understanding) was in thine heart."[57]

The Lord continued by providing a synopsis of how this endowment of understanding would manifest. He says it would make the king "wise and discerning."[58] Hence, we can logically assume the king not only had within him the ability to judge and discern matters of right and wrong concerning people and situations, but also matters of the ethereal nature of dreams, whether they were of God, of self, or of the netherworld.

> **Divine understanding is the critical key for both interpreting dreams and determining their origin.**

Although we don't see Solomon tasked explicitly with the burden of dream interpretation, we can assume that he possessed the ability to interpret because he had a heart full of wisdom and understanding from God. In the case of King Solomon, there is a beautiful tapestry of events that inaugurates Solomon's reign as king of Israel and establishes his unparalleled success.

It cannot be overstated that divine understanding is the critical key for both interpreting dreams and determining their origin. The Bible, as we have seen, gives numerous examples of men who received dreams

---

[57] 2 Chron 1:11, commentary added.
[58] 1 Kings 3:12, NASB

in the night from the Lord; however, to further explore the value of understanding, let us look once again at Daniel and his friends.

As for Daniel and his friends, they had the ability to understand spiritual things because the Bible says, "God gave them understanding." To ask for the skill of interpreting dreams is noble perhaps, but I think that desire is misguided. The better question should be, "God, will You give me an understanding heart so that I may benefit those who have dreams that come from You?" King Solomon, though he could've asked for many things from the Lord, asked God for a wise and understanding heart.

CHAPTER EIGHT

GOD'S WORD: OUR STANDARD FOR INTERPRETING DREAMS

I find the curiosity many people have in their dreams interesting. Most Christians I encounter have a bent to believing the dreams they have are either from God or are rooted in some sort of paranormal activity or encounter. People from near and far who have had a dream or series of dreams often approach me and ask for assistance in interpreting them.

While I appreciate that I would be considered reliable in the area of dreams and interpretation, it can be a bit concerning that, while so many are experiencing accelerated activity in the realms of dreams and visions of the night, so few have demonstrated an understanding of their dreams and an ability to interpret them.

> **There are ways to interpret dreams using the Scriptures as a filter, or the lens through which to understand various symbols seen in dreams.**

This, I believe, is evidence of one of two things: 1) a lack of the knowledge of the Word of God, or 2) an inability to employ the many nuances of Scripture, utilizing them as tools for dream interpretation. Nevertheless, both of these issues can be a catalyst for growth, either in spurring a hunger for the Word, or a desire to mature in the ability to use the Word as the roadmap for ascertaining what God is saying through dreams.

Even though dream symbolisms are often relevant to the time and culture in which we live, there are ways to interpret them using the Scriptures as a filter, or the lens through which to understand various symbols seen in dreams.

For example, a friend recently called and asked for help with interpreting a collection of dreams given to both him and another individual in his community. In the first dream, an airplane was seen flying at an extremely low altitude. The pilot of the plane could be clearly seen looking around and distracted, not knowing he was in danger of crashing into a building. The scene changes, and the dreamer was on a phone call with a family member who reported a plane had just crashed into their home. In the second dream, there was a shooting by an individual in their community.

After probing with several questions, I learned that during the same time these dreams were given, there was a divinely inspired increase of prayer during their gatherings, in which a certain leader in the church began seeing visions and having impressions of angelic activity during their meetings. Additionally, there was reportedly several new instances of shootings and other violent activities in the county where they lived, making their area statistically one of the most violent in their state. Upon hearing these cumulative dreams and other experiences, a few passages of Scripture came across my mind, and quickly the Lord gave the interpretation of the dreams.

In short, God was inviting this church community into an assignment of intercession to see the halting and reversing of violence released in their county. First, I was reminded of when Peter the apostle was chained in prison.[59] While the saints were praying for

---

[59] Acts 12:5-17, NASB

his release at a home gathering, the Angel of the Lord freed Peter from his chains. I knew what the Lord was saying through these dreams was that He was commissioning this community to intercession, and in so doing He was also ensuring that they would have angelic assistance.

The prophet Joel foretold of a coming day when the Lord would pour out His Spirit in a way that would transcend specific and special callings, and that the Spirit of God would unleash the gift of prophecy upon "all flesh."[60] What is of note is the way in which the Holy Spirit qualifies the distribution of the gift of prophecy given: "Your sons and your daughters shall prophesy, your **old men** shall ***dream dreams***, and your ***young men*** shall ***see visions***."

As we consider the two categories of "young men" and "old men," let us isolate the two groups with their prophetic gift sets given to them after the Spirit of God is poured out.

It is important to note the context of the prophesied outpouring is AFTER the people of God have gathered in solemnity, waiting on God through extended times of corporate prayer and fasting. Also, it is critical to view this prophetic promise in light of Acts chapter 2, where the Holy Spirit is poured upon

---

[60] Joel 2:28, NASB, emphasis added

the 120 disciples after a ten-day period of corporate prayer and fasting.

Afterwards, the apostle Peter quotes Joel chapter 2 verse 28 as the biblical explanation for what the disciples had just experienced in the Upper Room. He contextualized the Joel 2 verse by saying it would happen "in the last days," whereas the prophet uses the term "afterward" as the preposition for his prophecy.

As such, the Word of the Lord through Joel was for his day in the immediate sense, and for the Last Days in its widest application. The point here is, although Joel prophesied a coming outpouring, his initial utterance only gave a part of the whole understanding of God's mind, as did Peter's in Acts chapter 2.

YOUNG MEN SHALL SEE VISIONS

Usually when visions are spoken of in Christian circles, the understanding is that of an apparition, a trance-like experience, or encounter where one's "mind's eye" is opened and they are able to peer into the realm of the Spirit at some future event. These visions sometimes involve symbols, but more often can be direct intel with regard to the future.

These experiences are usually unintentional and without participation or interaction. However, I want to provide a more nuanced depiction of a vision, similar to what could be found in Daniel chapter 8, in which two important elements of visions can be seen in Daniel's experience: *contemplation* and *revelation*.

In Daniel chapter 8 verses 1 to 3, the prophet describes his encounter as having the vision *appear* unto him.[61] The Hebrew root for our English word "appear" is "ra'ah," which is most frequently translated as "to see" or "see," which has to do with the engagement of the physical eye in order to *gaze* or *behold* something or someone.

In the very next verse, however, the language seemingly begins to compound the experience of the vision, moving Daniel from simply beholding or gazing with the natural eye into employing his mental capacity for the purpose of gaining revelation and specificity relative to what he is beholding.

The word for vision is the Hebrew word "chazown" (pronounced Khaw-zone'), which is exclusively translated as "vision" with each use of the word. The word chazown literally means "a sight (mentally) i.e., a dream, revelation, or oracle." When understood, then, in context of the prophet Daniel's encounter, these two Hebrew words together give the picture of something appearing to the eyes, a subsequent process of contemplating the apparition, and resulting with the

---

[61] Dan 8:1-3, NASB

eventual apprehension of revelation or unveiling of deeper truths concealed within the apparition.

So then, Daniel would first "see" a thing with his physical or mental eyes, ponder the thing seen with consideration or contemplation of its meaning, and the Lord would unlock or unfold the mysterious significance of the visionary encounter or experience. This principle is not isolated to moments of ethereal encounters but can and should also be highly valued and engaged when approaching the written Word of God. It is often said that the Word of God is the primary place of encountering Him.

If this is the case—and indeed it is—the posture and mindset with which we approach the Scriptures can significantly impact the level of understanding, illumination, and revelatory insight we receive while spending time therein. Consider for example the book of the Revelation of Jesus Christ, which the apostle John wrote. Revelation chapter 1 verse 3 is a pronouncement of a blessing to anyone who reads, hears (understands), and does those things that are written in the prophecy.[62]

If a "blessing" is a "benefit" (an endowment which brings a good outcome) to a person, then it behooves anyone who reads the prophecy of the Revelation to

---

[62] Rev 1:3, NASB

position themselves in the best way possible to read, understand, and do what the prophecy reveals. Yet, the vast majority of Christians I know steer clear of reading the book of the Revelation altogether, because of the seemingly excessive usage of symbolic language.

An understanding I never knew existed became available to me only as I engaged the Scriptures with an honest, inquisitive heart and a fully engaged mind.

I believe the reason for this neglect is because for generations we have sought to filter the language of the Spirit through the lens of our extraordinarily limited Western understanding. Our efforts have acutely assembled a spiritual paradigm with a framework insufficient to house true ancient biblical concepts.

I, for one, was among the many who shunned the book of the Revelation of Jesus in my early days as a born-again Christian. However, as I applied myself to the consumption of and meditation in the Word of God, the words on the pages of the Bible began to "come alive," as it were, and an understanding I never knew existed became available to me only as I engaged the Scriptures with an honest, inquisitive heart and a fully engaged mind.

As I beheld the Scriptures, the Word of God Himself (let the reader understand) began to appear to me, even as He did to many of the patriarchs and prophets of antiquity. As phenomenal as this may sound, this way of visionary encounter through the Scriptures is a "standard issue" means of understanding. Illumination and revelation are available to the WHOLE church, and not relegated to those in a full-time ministry capacity.

So then, when the prophet Joel exclaims that young men would "see visions," these spiritual visionary encounters have to include those experiences that come by way of meditation in and contemplation of the Scriptures; encounters in which both the heart and mind come to the proverbial banqueting table of the Word with an honest and inquisitive appetite only to be quenched by feeding on the knowledge of God!

Young men and women who are postured in this way have access to a vast and limitless supply of satisfaction, which only comes by Spirit-given understanding, illumination, and revelation.

Decades of young men and women walking with God in this way produce old men and women well versed in the language of the Spirit and endowed with the spirit of wisdom and revelation. In the New Testament letter to Timothy, the apostle Paul tells his young understudy and son in the Gospel to "consider" what the apostle says, and as a consequence the Lord would give him understanding in ALL things![63]

What an unfathomable exchange! If we would with a ready mind and a willing heart consider (cogitate, ruminate, contemplate, ponder) what the Word says, the Lord would exponentially increase our level of understanding, illumination, and revelation! We MUST, however, be active participants in this process.

Even as I write this, I am reminded of one of the first God-given dream encounters I experienced as a new believer. In this encounter, I was on a ship in the middle of the ocean. The setting was at night, and the ship was apparently engulfed in a violent storm; the wind and waves battered the ship as the moonlit sky bore down on the vessel.

As I stood at the bow of the ship in the storm, a man that I understood to be the captain of the ship appeared to me, whose visage seemed as massive as the ship itself. He had piercing eyes, a little book in His hand, and was noticeably unaffected by the wind and waves beating against the vessel.

---

[63] 2 Tim 2:7, NASB

The man began to speak these words: "Blessed *is* the man that walketh not in the counsel of the ungodly, nor standeth in the way of sinners, nor sitteth in the seat of the scornful. But his delight *is* in the law of the Lord; and in his law doth he meditate day and night. And he shall be like a tree planted by the rivers of water, that bringeth forth his fruit in his season; his leaf also shall not wither; and whatsoever he doeth shall prosper."[64]

As I awakened from the dream, I was struck by two things: 1) I could remember verbatim the communication of the Man as if what He said to me was written on my heart and mind, and 2) I somehow knew what was said to me was written in the Bible. As a newly born-again believer I had very little knowledge of the Scriptures. However, when I opened my Bible, it somehow fell open to Psalm 1, which, to my utter amazement, was the exact same passage the Man in my dream had communicated to me! From then until now, I have no recollection of committing that passage of Scripture to memory and yet it is somehow indelibly lodged in my heart!

The eternal precept of meditation and contemplation in the Word of God is the key (I believe) to unlocking realms of insight and understanding things

---

[64] Ps 1:1-3, KJV

yet to be understood. As stated earlier, there are biblical examples of both Old and New Testament persons who engaged the invitations of God in this way, and consequently laid hold of things for which, until their time, there was no precedent. These same individuals serve as examples of how we should live, as well as models of how we can obtain fresh revelation knowledge in our day, which we so desperately need!

OLD MEN DREAM DREAMS

When it comes to the aged men and women dreaming dreams, the implications are many and massive. I submit that the reality of the old being dreamers is not relegated to them being physically fatigued and sleeping the sleep of death; rather, there is the reality of an awakened heart which is so well versed and exercised in the things of God that it has virtually no hinderances with regard to disseminating and interpreting the language of God given in the dream realm.

In his first epistle, the apostle John explains to his readers his reasons for which he had written to them, and he provides for us two contributory predicates for why he writes, with references to three specific groups of readers to whom he writes: *little children*, *young men*, and *fathers*.

To the *little children* he explains the purpose of his writing to them is because their sins are forgiven. This purpose, though vitally and crucially important to understand, is a foundational doctrine found at the base of the Gospel message. And though it is absolutely necessary, it is elementary as far as the knowledge of God is concerned. Though God never changes, to the finite human mind the understanding of Him is eternally dynamic and progressive.

> **Though God never changes, to the finite human mind the understanding of Him is eternally dynamic and progressive.**

To the *young men* the aged apostle affirms their youthful vitality and subsequent ability to subdue the wicked one because of the Word of God in them. With the exercise of the Word, the young man builds strength, endurance, and skill sufficient to grapple with and subjugate the enemy of their soul.

Lastly, to the *fathers* the aged apostle affirms their experiential advantage, emphasizing their knowledge of God and of His ways. In other words, their history with God gave them advantages that mere mortal strength can never afford. It is akin to the statement the psalmist made concerning the difference in Moses and the rest of Israel relative to their understanding of Jehovah: "He made known his ways (thoughts and reasonings) unto Moses, his acts (power and authority) unto the children of Israel."[65]

IS THIS GOD?

One of the most important and often most miscalculated issues relative to dreams and interpretation is the dream source. The ability to ascertain where the dream came from is perhaps as important as the dream itself. Not every dream is from the Spirit of God, and thus, should not be given the same weight or gravity.

There are some dream encounters that leave no doubt as to the source. Often those are the ones where either the Lord's voice is made known, the message is direct, or there is little to no symbolism. In such experiences, there is often a divine instruction or clear revelation of the Word.

A biblical example is found in Daniel chapter 7 verses 15 through 16. In the midst of this dream encounter, Daniel engaged an individual and asked for the meaning of the dream and vision upon his bed. The account is as follows:

> "I, Daniel, was troubled in spirit, and the visions that passed through my mind disturbed

---
[65] Ps 103:7, KJV, emphasis added

me. I approached one of those standing there and asked him the meaning of all this. So, he told me and gave me the interpretation of these things."[66]

Daniel had direct access to the dream's understanding while still IN THE DREAM. Though his human understanding was limited, he was given divine assistance while in the state of dreaming, so that when he awoke, the knowledge of God through the dream was imparted to him. So then, often when a dream is from the Lord, He imparts the knowledge of the dream in our hearts and minds so as to engraft it into our soul.

Often when a dream is from the Lord, He imparts the knowledge of the dream in our hearts and minds so as to engraft it into our soul.

I have personally experienced dreams, such as the one mentioned earlier, where the information was imparted to me to the extent that I remember every detail twenty years later. I didn't need to write it, because it became an indelible part of me. However, over the course of the last twenty-two or so years since salvation, I can only recall a handful of dreams that

---

[66] Dan 7:15-16, NIV

came to me in that way. Most frequently the dreams we experience are soon forgotten, unless we employ the stewardship of journaling.

One other biblical example of God-given dreams is one in which the dream is repetitive. As stated earlier, in the days of Joseph the pharaoh of Egypt experienced such dreams, wherein the dreams were successive with a slight variation of content and use of symbolisms. Notice in particular the response of Joseph upon hearing the series of dreams: "God has shown to Pharaoh what He is about to do...as for the repeating of the dream to Pharaoh twice, *it means* that the matter is determined by God."[67]

Because of Joseph's lifelong experience in dreams and interpretation, he developed a philosophy of understanding not only the meaning of dreams, but also their origins by way of delivery. In other words, Joseph understood the dreams to be from God both because of their successive and repetitive nature, and the interpolation of symbols.

Additionally, Joseph understood that God was communicating His plans and intentions to Pharaoh due to the nature or tenure of details in the dreams. As such, Joseph (and consequently Pharaoh) regarded the dreams as being from the Lord.

---

[67] Gen 41:25, 32, NASB

That is not to say that all dreams with a certain set of symbolisms are divine; one must take care not to assume such things. In fact, all human language is built upon the use and association of symbols. Creation itself has elements of symbolism, which God specifically designed for that reason alone: "to be for signs."[68]

> **One sure way to determine the source of a dream is to simply ask, "Holy Spirit, is this You?"**

All in all, dreams that are more symbolic in nature need decoding or interpreting in order for there to be understanding. But at the end of the day, one sure way to determine the source of a dream is to simply ask, "Holy Spirit, is this You?"

God is eager to impart of Himself to mankind, and speaking through dreams is certainly not the least of means by which He does so. In His infinite mercy, God released a dream, a communication of divine intelligence, to a man who was not only godless, but who also considered himself to be God and demanded the worship of his people. Yet the Most High God imparted knowledge of future events through the most unlikely source, and preserved life in the midst of a catastrophic global famine.

---

[68] Gen 1:14, NASB

We know dreams are not unique to the Church, even revelatory dreams. There are several accounts of common individuals (let the reader understand) who have had dreams of various things, including "visions" of future events. However, we must draw a distinction between that which is from the soul and what is of the Spirit.

Because the soul is eternal, it is quite possible—and perhaps even normal—to have dream experiences of the abnormal sort. The human soul has the potential to experience things in the unseen realm because the soul itself is of the same substance. The difference is the source of the experience.

The writer of Hebrews reminds us of the work of the Scriptures, which is to discern and divide between soul and spirit, as well as the heart's thoughts and intentions. Hence, a heart and life rooted in the knowledge of God through the Word is our roadmap to knowing what is of God and what is of the human soul.

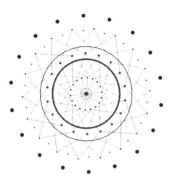

CHAPTER NINE

FROM JOEL 2 TO ACTS 2

At the outset of this writing, it was not my intention to simply survey the Scriptures and harvest revelation concerning dreams. However, while doing so, it has become clearer than ever that God still intends to fulfill the exceeding great and precious promises of His Word, especially as the end of the age so quickly approaches. One particular promise yet unfolding is the prophetic utterance of Joel chapter 2 verses 28 and 29: "And it shall come to pass ***afterward*** that I will pour out My Spirit on all flesh; Your sons and your daughters shall prophesy, Your old men shall dream dreams, Your young men shall see visions. And also, on *My* menservants and on *My* maidservants, I will pour out My Spirit ***in those days***."[69]

What strikes me as peculiar is the use of terms such as "afterward" and "in those days." As noted earlier, Peter, the great apostle and most prominent disciple, used this very passage to give articulation and explanation to the Upper Room encounter in the day (singular) the Holy Spirit and fire descended upon the 120. In the apostle's proclamation, however, he interpreted the prophecy of Joel as being an ongoing "Last Days" reality rather than a once-in-a-lifetime event in history. That being the case, the outpouring of the Spirit is just as relevant today than it has ever been.

In context, the people of God are being assembled together for the expressed purpose of sanctification, and it is that very dynamic that qualifies the Church for receiving such an outpouring of the Spirit, as indicated in Joel chapter 2 verses 15 through 17:

> "Blow the trumpet in Zion, consecrate a fast, call a sacred assembly; Gather the people, Sanctify the congregation, Assemble the elders, Gather the children and nursing babes; Let the bridegroom go out from his chamber, And the bride from her dressing room. Let the priests,

---
[69] Joel 2:28-29, NKJV. emphasis added

who minister to the Lord, Weep between the porch and the altar."[70]

It is only after the people of God respond to a certain call to action that God Himself responds out of heaven to the posture of the people. Joel chapter 2 verse 28 and Acts chapter 2 is such a response. Moreover, if the principle of Joel 2 was relevant in the days of Acts 2, it is logical to conclude it is indeed relevant still today.

Principles do not change, conditions do, and the condition of the Church in the West is in such a state that warrants a trumpet call back to sanctification, which can only come by way of national corporate fasting and prayer! If this becomes the reality in the Church, then ***afterward***, as God promised through His prophet, there will be a response from heaven, an outpouring of the Spirit and power of God upon the sanctified Church.

God will be in the midst and will begin to lead His people again, and as a byproduct of the fullness of the Spirit within us, He will send dreams and visions as a means to both navigate unknown terrains of life and to be a prophetic witness unto Him in the earth!

Afterward is critical, in that it denotes a point in time where something is at hand because of what has

---

[70] Joel 2:15-17, NKJV

already come to pass; it is the hinge of the door to the eternal possibilities of God. ***Afterward*** is an invitation to consecration; the cessation of self and self-reliance for the purpose of inviting and retaining God in the midst.

The dying of one's self and the end of all self-reliance is the ONLY way to ensure the great outpouring of the Spirit upon the people of God.

People of God, consecration—the dying of one's self and the end of all self-reliance in order that the divine Life and purposes of God might prevail—is the ONLY way to ensure the great outpouring of the Spirit upon the people of God as promised in Joel chapter 2 and Acts chapter 2. Actually, it is key to determining the difference between the dreams of the heavenly realm and that which is of the realm of the self.

The promise of the great outpouring of the Spirit is indeed predicated upon the ability of God's people to wholeheartedly embrace self-denial and walk the way of the Cross. This "way" is the highway of God, the landing strip upon which the Holy Spirit descends and remains. Divine dreams and visions are merely a byproduct of a holy God having revealed Himself to His holy people.

As emphasized in earlier portions of this writing, the realm of dreams is an avenue by which the sovereign

Lord makes Himself known to whomever He chooses. He says, in fact, "I will speak...in a dream"[71] to those He regards as prophetic people.

In the preceding verses we see the desire of the heart of God expressed through Moses is that ALL of the people of God would be as prophets. If this is true (and it indeed is), then it can be concluded that God desires to speak to ALL of His people in dreams! Would to God that we would position ourselves in corporate consecration, so as to be a people of His pleasure! Would to God that He would bend toward us and extend to us the divine language of dreams, the bridge that translates us from mere human experience into the realms of heavenly realities and the knowledge of God!

I feel strongly that a renewed emphasis on this area of divine dreams is being released into the earth, and that the WHOLE CHURCH, regardless of denominational and philosophical leanings, is being invited by the sovereign Lord to partake of this great fellowship of God and His people. I feel strongly the charge to once again respond in faith to this invitation by consecrating ourselves and purifying our lives so that our spiritual ears are tuned to hear as the Dream Speaker pours forth the mysteries of Himself and leads His Church through dreams in the night.

---

[71] Num 12:6, NASB

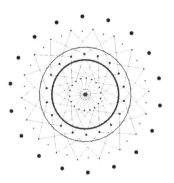

AFTERWORD

This little excerpt at the end of my friend Corry Robinson's epic book on dreams is what they call an *afterword*. I think it is fitting that isn't a foreword because there is an "afterword" that is critical to the understanding of the last days' global outpouring of dreams and visions.

In Joel 2, we hear the sounding of a prophetic trumpet, calling for united fasting and prayer in the last days' crises of nations. Following that fast, Joel 2:28 declares, "And it shall come to pass *afterward*, that I will pour out My Spirit on all flesh. Your sons and your daughters shall prophesy, your old men shall dream dreams, your young men shall see visions, and also on My menservants and my maidservants I will pour out My Spirit in those days." Clearly, there is a connection between the massive infusion of heaven's dreams into the earth and the last days' calling to fasting. So, in this afterword, I join with the trumpet call of this book and declare there is a *foreword* for the *afterword*. The foreword is fasting, and the afterword is dreams.

The message transferred to us in this book erupted out of a forty-day fast that God had called Corry into.

For thirty-five years I have given myself to God in seasons of extended fasting, and in almost every period of extended fasting, I and my prophetic friends have received dreams from heaven that unveil God's love, His benevolent corrections, and divine blueprints for the next assignments in our lives. This is stunning! Fasting makes your life a landing strip for prophetic revelation.

What's remarkable to me is the message transferred to us in this book erupted out of a forty-day fast that God had called Corry into. In fact, Joel prophesies of a last days period when all flesh, male and female, believer and unbeliever, young and old, will be invaded with dreams so real. In every life (all flesh), there will be a stairway to heaven, in which angels ascend and descend, declaring the messages of God's heart in dreams, because fasting has cleared the skies

AFTERWORD

of demonic interference and cleansed the highways of human hearts.

Years ago, I had a conversation with a schoolteacher asking the question, "Why do we pray for Muslims to have dreams of Jesus and not for our kids in our suburban schools?" Right there we prayed that God would give a dream the next day to a student in my friend's school where he taught.

The following day a student came up to him and said, "Mr. Harris, I had a dream last night that I was giving my life to Jesus! My friend asked, "Well, did you do it?" The young man said, "No." "Would you like to?" my friend responded. The young man right then and there gave his life to Jesus.

ALL FLESH will dream dreams. Oh, that the Church worldwide would ask, seek, and knock on the doors of heaven for the end-time gift of dreams. "How much more will your heavenly Father give good gifts to those who ask?"

When Corry told me about his vision of equipping the earth in the last days' language of dreams, my heart leapt. This has to be done! I believe Corry, in his book, is at the cutting edge of an unfolding drama of God's dreams coming to the earth. I told Corry, "I want to do this with you." You have heard of DreamWorks, but I want to declare, "Dreams work!"

My son Jonathan received a dream that he was finding his "theater of dreams." What language! A theater is where you act out a playscript and God is the scriptwriter, and many times act 1, act 2, act 3, and so on, are revealed to us in dreams. But a dream received and not acted on remains only a dream.

> **How often we pass by our burning bushes because we don't pause and ponder the divine dream that's wrapped in the swaddling clothes of heaven's simple symbolism.**

For years people have told me their dreams, saying, "It's just a dream," or, "It was just a short dream." My response is always, "Just a dream? Who knows what angels had to fight through to deliver the message?" If dreams are indeed the last days' language of the Holy Spirit, according to Joel 2:28, then there needs to be a great revaluation of them. In other words, we need to reassess great value to dreams and not say that they are part of a subconscious stew brewing within our sleep.

We need a biblical return to the sense of the sacred in dreams. How often we pass by our burning bushes because we don't pause and ponder the divine dream that's wrapped in the swaddling clothes of heaven's simple symbolism. Like Jesus' parables of old, understanding is hidden to the cynical and unbelieving.

AFTERWORD

When we turn aside and gaze at that wonderful vision of the night, we may hear our name being called and take off our shoes to find ourselves standing on holy ground.

Abraham Heschel said, "More is learned in one moment of awe than in a lifetime of calculation." In this light, I appeal to you, having read this amazing book, unshackle yourself from the chains of unbiblical rationality and allow yourself to experience a measure of awe of the God who speaks. Like Jacob, when he had a dream, let us say, "How awesome is this place! This is none other than the gate of heaven and the house of God!" We need an Awe-Wakening.

Judge these words you have read to see if they align with Scripture and if they witness to your spirit. If they do, then renounce a casual approach to the prophetic. If you find yourself stirred by this book, move beyond awe to action. Live a life of extended fasting. Ask and seek for dreams and then step into a lifelong adventure of the liberating flight and revelation by letting dreams give you wings into a new era in your life. I believe that most dreams are actually windows through which the whole earth is gazing and yearning for the future reign of Christ. Let dreams come, let the Kingdom come!

Lou Engle, Founder and President
Lou Engle Ministries

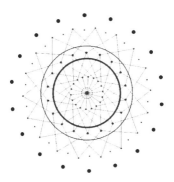

ABOUT THE AUTHOR

Corry is an intercessor, worship leader, preacher, and author with a prophetic calling. While pursuing a career in the secular music industry as a signed artist to a major recording label, Corry abandoned the industry after encountering the glory of God in a church gathering he was invited to at age twenty-two. There he committed himself to a consecrated life in response to the call of God. Since that time, Corry has served as an elder in the local church and has ministered internationally with a burning desire to see men and women changed by the glory of God, yielding themselves as vessels fit for His divine purposes. Corry is married to Lakisha, the love of his life, with whom he resides in Orlando, Florida, and serves the church locally.